D1178845

PUPPYDOGS

PUPPYDOGS

a photographic celebration

MQP
MQ Publications Ltd

A dog may be man's best

friend, but a child's best

friend is a puppy.

Unknown

The fidelity of a dog is a precious gift.

Konrad Lorenz

One reason a dog can be

such a comfort when you're

feeling blue is that he doesn't

try to find out why.

Unknown

Buy a pup and your

money will buy love

unflinching.

Rudyard Kipling

I am called a dog because I fawn on those who give me anything, I yelp at those who refuse, and I set my teeth in rascals.

Diogenes

If you would invest in friendship,

purchase a dog.

Le Baron Cooke

Rambunctious, rumbustious,

delinquent dogs become

angelic when sitting.

Dr Ian Dunbar

Money will buy you a pretty good dog,

but it won't buy the wag of its tail.

Josh Billings

Like a dog, he hunts in dreams.

Alfred, Lord Tennyson

Dogs are not our whole life,

but they make our lives whole.

Roger Caras

I've seen a look in dogs' eyes, a quickly

vanishing look of amazed contempt,

and I am convinced that basically dogs

think humans are nuts.

John Steinbeck

My little dog,

a heartbeat at my feet.

Edith Wharton

I cannot impress on my readers too strongly the necessity to be firm but kind to a puppy. His idea of your authority is forming, and if he knows you give in on the slightest whimper, you are wacked for life.

Barbara Woodhouse

No animal should ever jump up on the living

room furniture unless absolutely certain he

can hold his own in the conversation.

Fran Lebowitz

The censure of a dog is something no man can stand.

Christopher Morley

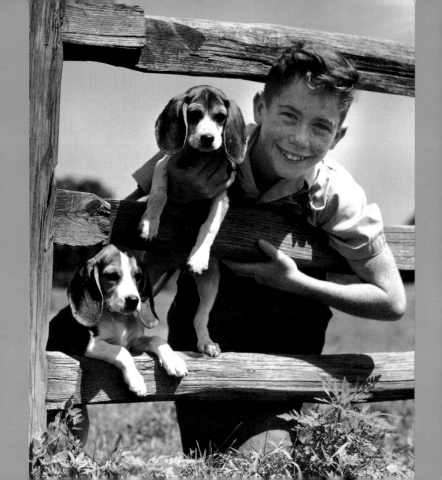

The dog is a gentleman;

I hope to go to his heaven,

not man's.

Mark Twain

Bulldogs are adorable,

with faces like toads

that have been sat on.

Colette

There will always be a lost little

dog somewhere that will prevent

me from being happy.

Jean Anouilh

The best way

to get a puppy is to

beg for a baby brother—

and they'll settle for a

puppy every time.

Winston Pendelton

Life is like a dogsled team.

If you ain't the lead dog,

the scenery never changes.

Lewis Grizzard

Dogs are our link to paradise. They don't know evil or jealousy or discontent. To sit with a dog on a hillside on a glorious afternoon is to be back in Eden, where doing nothing was not boring—it was peace.

Milan Kundera

I myself have known some

profoundly thoughtful dogs.

James Thurber

I hope my tongue in prune juice smothers

If I belittle dogs and mothers.

Ogden Nash

It is fatal to let any dog know that he

is funny, for he immediately loses his

head and starts hamming it up.

P. G. Wodehouse

Then drink, puppy, drink, and let every puppy drink.

G. J. Whyte-Melville

It's a dog's life.

English saying

A puppy plays with every pup he meets,

but an old dog has few associates.

Josh Billings

If a dog will not come to you

having looked you in the face,

you should go home and

examine your conscience.

Woodrow Wilson

Children and dogs are as necessary to the welfare

of the country as Wall Street and the railroads.

Harry S Truman

Every dog must have his day.

Jonathan Swift

I never saw such a bouncing,

swaggering puppy since I was born.

Oliver Goldsmith

It's impossible to keep a straight face in

the presence of one or more puppies.

Unknown

No matter what you've done

wrong, always try to make it

look like the dog did it.

Unknown

The dog was created specially for children.

He is the god of frolic.

Henry Ward Beecher

Extraordinary creature!

So close a friend,

yet so remote.

Thomas Mann

He that would hang his dog

gives out first that he is mad.

English proverb

Puppies are nature's remedy for feeling unloved…

plus numerous other ailments of life.

Richard Allan Palm

Men are generally more careful of

the breed of their horses and dogs

than of their children.

William Penn

If you eliminate smoking and gambling, you will be amazed to find that almost all an Englishman's pleasures can be, and mostly are, shared by his dog.

George Bernard Shaw

The biggest dog has been a pup.

Joaquin Miller

No man can be condemned for owning a dog.

As long as he has a dog, he has a friend.

Will Rogers

If you are a dog and

your owner suggests

you wear a sweater,

suggest he wears a tail.

Fran Lebowitz

The disposition of a noble dog is to be

gentle with people they know and the

opposite with those they don't know.

Plato

Whoever said you can't buy

happiness forgot little puppies.

Gene Hill

If a picture
wasn't going
very well, I'd
put a puppy
dog in it.

Norman Rockwell

TALE!

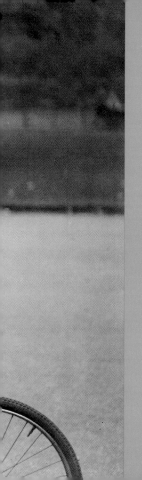

Even a dog we do know

is better company than

a man whose language

we do not know.

Saint Augustine

Dogs are getting bigger,

according to a leading dog manufacturer.

Leo Rosten

In order to really enjoy a dog, one doesn't merely try to train him to be semi-human. The point of it is to open oneself to the possibility of becoming partly a dog.

Edward Hoagland

You think dogs will not be in heaven?

I tell you, they will be there long before any of us.

Robert Louis Stevenson

If it wasn't for puppies, some

people would never go for a walk.

Anonymous

Dogs have not the power of comparing.

A dog will take a small piece of meat as readily as a

large, when both are before him.

Samuel Johnson

When a puppy wags its tail and

barks at the same time, how do you

know which end to believe?

Anonymous

No matter how little money and

how few possessions you own,

having a dog makes you rich.

Louis Sabin

Picture Credits

All images Hulton Getty Picture Collection.

cover: A Great Dane at the Kensington Canine Society's dog show, London, 1933.

title page: Four Samoyed puppies riding in the pram of four-year-old Shirley Neale, London, 1937.

page 5: A small boy sits on a lawn petting a puppy, circa 1955. Lambert/Hulton Archive.

page 6/7: A woman kissing a puppy, circa 1950. International Centre of Photography/Hulton Archive

page 9: A sad-looking boy sits on a step cuddling a puppy, circa 1945. Esther Henderson/Hulton Archive.

page 10: American actor Tuesday Weld with her puppy, Marco. LaGuardia Airport, New York, 1963.

page 13: A boy posts a sign on a fence, watched by his terrier puppies, circa 1945. Lambert/Hulton Archive.

page 14/15: A young boy and a basset hound puppy in a toy car, circa 1955. Lambert/Hulton Archive.

page 16/17: Irish setter puppies, 1946. Morgan Collection/Hulton Archive.

page 18: A little girl pulling along her toy puppy on a string in a park, 1930.

page 20/21: Swedish foxhound pups, 1972.

page 22/23: Actress Renée Adorée with a litter of puppies born on the set of her film "Rose Marie," 1928.

page 25: Five red dachshunds at Crufts, UK, 1971.

page 26: Connie Hutchin taking her tiny Yorkshire terrier for a walk, London, 1964.

page 29: Police Constable David Marvin clutching some red setter puppies, 1946.

page 30: This puppy is smaller than a telephone, 1978.

page 33: A forlorn-looking Cairn terrier on a stool, 1933.

page 34: A boy and his beagle puppies look through a fence, circa 1955. Lambert/Hulton Archive.

page 37: A bulldog puppy named Mitch after Robert Mitchum, 2000.

page 38: Marion Davies stars in "Peg O' My Heart," 1933. John Kobal Foundation/Hulton Archive.

page 41: A young hunt follower makes friends with beagle pups too young to join in the hunt, 1938.

page 42: Pet husky dogs owned by the Webb family of Blue Mountain Lake, New York, circa 1955.

page 44/45: Two young boys lie in the grass with a puppy, circa 1955. Lambert/Hulton Archive.

page 46: A dalmatian puppy peers out nervously from a large wicker basket, 1939.

page 48: Entrants to the King Charles Spaniel Club show, London, 1928.

page 51: A black puppy in a Halloween costume, circa 1945. John Zavisho/Hulton Archive.

Published by MQ Publications Limited
12 The Ivories, 6–8 Northampton Street, London, N1 2HY
Tel: 020 7359 2244 / Fax: 020 7359 1616
e-mail: mail@mqpublications.com

ISBN: 1-84072-318-1

1 3 5 7 9 0 8 6 4 2

Cover design: John Casey
Design: Philippa Jarvis

Printed and bound in China